VIKINGS

Moira Butterfield

W
FRANKLIN WATTS
LONDON•SYDNEY

Franklin Watts
First published in Great Britain in 2017 by The Watts Publishing Group

Credits
Series Editor: John C. Miles
Series Designer: Richard Jewitt
Picture researcher: Diana Morris
Picture Credits: ATG Images/Shutterstock: 19tr. D M Cherry/Shutterstock: 21tr. Chris Coe/Visit
Britain Getty Images: 18-19. Copora/Dreamstime: 9tr. Gunnar Creutz/CC Wikimedia: back cover
tl. Derby Museums/Richard Tailby: 7c, 7tr. Corey A Ford/Dreamstime: 1, 5tr. Gallo Images/Getty
Images: front cover c, 5c. Granger NYC/Alamy: 27c. Angelo Hornak/Alamy: 28-29c. Ying Feng
Johansson/Dreamstime: 25tr. Jorisvo/Dreamstime: 29tr. Manx National Museum: 17c. Cindy Miller
Hopkins/Alamy: 11tr. Nachosan/CC Wikimedia: back cover br. National Museums Scotland: 10-11c.
Portable Antiquities Scheme BY-SA: 22-23. Saile 76/Dreamstime: 17tr. Sponner/Shutterstock: 23tr.
Ben Stanshall/Getty Images: 9c. Stocksolutions/Dreamstime: 27tr. Charles Tait: 25c. Published to
Wikimedia Commons with the explicit permission of Jon Haylett , author of A Kilchoan Diary: 20-21.
York Archaeological Trust: 12-13c, 13tr, 14-15c, 15tr,

HB ISBN 978 1 4451 5296 7
PB ISBN 978 1 4451 5297 4

Printed in China

MIX
Paper from
responsible sources
FSC® C104740
FSC
www.fsc.org

Franklin Watts
An imprint of
Hachette Children's Group
Part of The Watts Publishing Group
Carmelite House
50 Victoria Embankment
London EC4Y 0DZ

An Hachette UK Company
www.hachette.co.uk

www.franklinwatts.co.uk

CONTENTS

Attack! – Lindisfarne Priory Stone   4

Here to stay – Repton Great Army   6

Caught by enemies – The Weymouth Massacre   8

Farming Vikings – Jarlshof   10

A busy workplace – Coppergate   12

Viking style – Jorvik clothing   14

A Viking wise woman – The Lady of Peel   16

A Viking parliament – Tynwald Hill   18

A Viking leader – Ardnamurchan ship grave   20

Hidden treasure – Silverdale Hoard   22

Reading the runes – Maeshowe   24

Viking pictures – St. Paul's Rune Stone   26

A new God – Horn of Ulf   28

Glossary   30

Further information and Timeline   31

Index   32

Attack!
LINDISFARNE PRIORY STONE

793
Date of the attack

DATE FOUND:
AROUND 1900,
IN AMONGST
RUBBLE.

From the end of the 700s, pirate gangs from Scandinavia began attacking the coast of Britain. They stole anything they could carry back home to sell, including church treasures and slaves. We call these attackers the Vikings. Their first recorded attack came in 793 when they made a lightning raid on the monastery of Lindisfarne. A gravestone from the site gives us a clue to how frightening the Vikings were.

PLACE FOUND:
LINDISFARNE,
NORTHUMBERLAND.

The monastery was destroyed when the Vikings struck. It was later rebuilt and the gravestone, called the Priory Stone, was found by archaeologists in amongst the rubble of later ruins. We don't know who the gravestone was for, but it is carved with a picture that shows the Viking attack. It shows the attackers carrying swords and axes.

The Vikings launched their raid from swift narrow boats called longships, which they sailed across the North Sea. Monks who later wrote about the attack said the Vikings raided Lindisfarne in mid-January. North Sea sailing conditions would have been very rough at that time of year, so perhaps the Vikings arrived weeks earlier and lurked further up the coast, spying out a good target.

Longships were powered by oars or by a square sail, shown on this imagined picture. The prow was sometimes carved in the shape of a dragon, to impress and scare anyone who saw it.

The monastery would have had treasures, such as silver altar candles and precious handwritten books with jewelled covers. The Vikings would have prised off the jewels with their daggers and snatched the silver to hack up and use as money. They would have grabbed people to sell as slaves, too.

Fleeing monks spread news of the raid. It shocked everyone and monks described the attackers as 'stinging hornets' and 'hungry wolves'. Vikings, famed for their brutality with swords and axes (as shown on the stone), launched many terrifying hit-and-run raids over the next 200 years.

The people who lived in England at this time were called the Anglo-Saxons. They were Christians, whereas the Vikings were pagans who believed in their own gods and goddesses. They wouldn't have cared about destroying churches and stealing holy objects from the Anglo-Saxons.

What would you do if you were standing on the shore and you saw a Viking longship approaching?

Here to stay
REPTON GREAT ARMY

In 865 the Vikings changed their tactics. Instead of simply raiding and leaving, they decided to stay in Britain and take over land. A large band we call the Great Army arrived from Denmark and rampaged across the country for 14 years, fighting in summer and camping in winter. One of their winter camps has been rediscovered in Derbyshire, where a warrior died of his battle wounds and was buried ready for a trip to the Viking afterlife.

873
Date of the winter camp

DATE FOUND: 1988, BY ARCHAEOLOGISTS.

PLACE FOUND: REPTON DERBYSHIRE.

We know that the Vikings camped at Repton because it was mentioned in Anglo-Saxon writings of the time. Archaeologists investigating the site discovered that the Vikings made their headquarters and buried their dead in and around an Anglo-Saxon church they had taken over. Amongst the dead was a warrior who had died from terrible sword wounds. By studying the shape of his skull, experts were able to make a model of his head (they guessed that he had blue eyes and a beard).

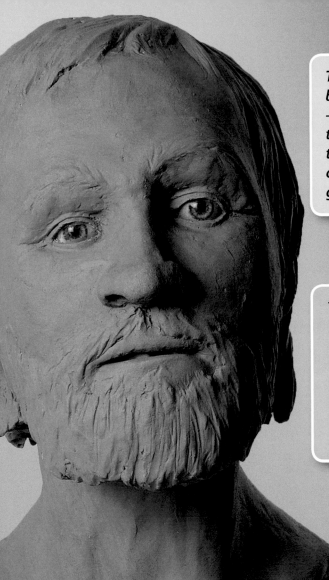

The Repton warrior was buried with a silver amulet – a lucky charm similar to this one. It was shaped like the hammer believed to be carried by Thor, the Viking god of thunder.

This is the reconstructed head of the warrior from Repton. He was killed by sword blows to his head and body. He probably died fighting against Anglo-Saxons from the local kingdom of Mercia.

An even bigger winter camp has been uncovered at Torksey in Lincolnshire. It was used by the Great Army the year before they camped at Repton. Thousands of Vikings camped there on a site the size of 75 football pitches. We know from objects found there that they spent the winter repairing weapons, ships and clothing and even making jewellery.

Viking warriors who died in battle were believed to become immortal and go to a feasting hall called Valhalla in the kingdom of Asgard, home of the Viking gods and goddesses. The warrior was buried with the things he needed to take to Valhalla. His sword was laid beside him in a wooden fleece-lined scabbard.

The warrior had the Thor hammer as a lucky charm. What lucky charms do you have?

Caught by enemies
THE WEYMOUTH MASSACRE

By 880 the Vikings had taken much of northern and eastern England and controlled an area called the Danelaw. An uneasy truce with the Anglo-Saxons didn't last and violence broke out again in the 900s. A mass grave of Viking men found in Dorset tells a grisly story of those dangerous times.

970
Approximate date

DATE FOUND: 2009, DURING A ROAD-BUILDING PROJECT.

PLACE FOUND: RIDGEWAY HILL, WEYMOUTH, DORSET.

Digging during a road project at Ridgeway Hill, on the edge of Weymouth, unearthed 54 male skeletons in an old quarry pit. The victims all had their heads cut off in a horrific mass execution. Archaeologists used forensic science techniques to study the bones, just as police do in modern crime cases. They discovered that the men were Vikings but we don't know who killed them. It could have been the Anglo-Saxons or even other enemy Vikings.

Most of the victims were men between the ages of 18 and 25. They were executed next to a well-used track, the equivalent of a main road in modern times. They had no clothes or belongings buried with them.

None of the victims had armour, but we know from other remains that Viking fighters did not wear horned helmets, as once thought. Their helmets looked like this reconstruction.

Analysis of the teeth from the massacre show that all the victims came from different parts of Scandinavia or Russia. Some of the teeth had been filed down by their owners to make horizontal grooves that would have been filled with coloured paste. It was a fashion among warriors of the time to have striped teeth. You can see grooves on the teeth in this skull.

At around the time the men were killed, Anglo-Saxons from the kingdom of Wessex, in the south of England, had fought back and regained territory from the Vikings. But war bands were once again coming over from Scandinavia. They even besieged and burnt London.

The way that some of the skeletal bones were shaped suggests that some of the executed men had spent long hours rowing, so it's possible that some of the victims were the crew of a longship.

Find out if any Vikings invaded near where you live.

Farming Vikings
JARLSHOF

Once Vikings conquered land they settled it with their families, growing crops and keeping animals to feed themselves. A Viking farm has been uncovered at Jarlshof on the southern tip of the island of Mainland in Shetland, Scotland. The occupants left behind some fascinating clues about Viking life, including some doodles on pieces of slate (rock).

800-1100
Date of slate picture

DATE FOUND:
VIKING FARM EXCAVATED 1930S TO 1950S.

PLACE FOUND:
JARLSHOF, MAINLAND, SHETLAND.

Over a hundred years ago a storm washed away earth at Jarlshof, revealing mysterious stone walls. The first remains found after the storm belonged to far older times than the Viking era, but in the following decades archaeologists discovered Viking homes and belongings there. The Scandinavians probably arrived by sea and took over the site from local people, called Picts, who lived there before them.

There were several Viking houses at Jarlshof. Related families probably lived in them, working together to feed themselves. They grew crops and caught fish, and they kept farm animals for meat, milk and skins. We know from bones left behind that a small terrier dog once lived at Jarlshof, too.

Among the Viking belongings left behind there was a game board of squares scratched on a piece of slate, along with some pebble game pieces. There were even some tiny toys, carved from stone, in the shape of a bowl and corn-grinding stones. Perhaps the Viking child who owned them used to play at cooking.

A Viking home was called a longhouse because it was long and narrow. Inside everyone lived together in one room, sleeping on benches covered in animal skins.

Several pictures and patterns were found scratched on pieces of slate on the farm. One of them, shown here, is a drawing of a longship with a high prow and stern, oars and a steering paddle at the back.

The Jarlshof families would have spent their evenings sitting around a fire in their homes, spinning wool, making tools or listening to someone telling sagas – mythical stories of Viking heroes and monsters. Perhaps somebody made the slate doodles while they sat by the fire.

What would you like and dislike about living in a longhouse?

A busy workplace
COPPERGATE

The Vikings made York the capital of their territory in the north. They called it Jorvik. In an area of town now called Coppergate there were lots of workshops where people made goods of all kinds to sell. Archaeologists have uncovered thousands of objects from Coppergate, telling the story of Vikings busy at their daily work.

866-954
Years when Vikings controlled Jorvik (York)

DATE FOUND:
MAIN EXCAVATION,
1976 TO 1981.

PLACE FOUND:
YORK,
YORKSHIRE.

In 1972 local archaeologists dug a couple of trenches in a pavement outside a local high street bank. They found Viking objects scattered deep in the underground soil, everything well preserved because of the dampness of the earth. In 1976 work began on a much bigger dig that turned up lots of everyday objects, from pottery pieces

The wooden bowls and cups shown here were made in a Coppergate wood-turning workshop. There were also workshops for blacksmiths, jewellers, glass-blowers, leather workers and bone carvers.

The wooden cups shown here were probably used for beer, a popular Viking drink. The bowls would have held typical Viking food, such as a stew of boiled meat bones, beans and vegetables.

Some of the objects from Jorvik are hard to identify. This mysterious fragment of carved bone might come from a musical instrument or perhaps a hairpin, but we don't know for sure. It shows a monster swallowing two birds.

Archaeologists found the preserved bodies of fleas and lice that would once have made the Viking locals itch as they worked! The damp Coppergate soil even preserved Viking poo and the moss and wool fragments used as toilet paper.

When the Vikings first arrived in Britain they paid for things with scraps of silver, called hack silver, weighed to see how much it was worth. Eventually they copied the local Anglo-Saxons and started making their own coins. Some of these have turned up at Coppergate, along with coin-making equipment.

Find out if there are craftspeople who make things near where you live. What do they make?

Viking style
JORVIK CLOTHING

Beautifully preserved Viking shoes were found at the Coppergate dig in York, along with a selection of brooches. They are rare examples of the type of clothing that Vikings wore in Britain.

Between
866-954
Date the Vikings lived in Jorvik

DATE FOUND:
1976 TO 1981, DURING EXCAVATIONS.

PLACE FOUND:
YORK, YORKSHIRE.

The finds at Coppergate tell us that it would have been a good place to go shopping for fashion. Shoppers could buy a new pair of shoes or get old ones repaired. They could choose items such as a new leather belt, a useful pouch or a new brooch. They could buy amber beads brought all the way from the Baltic or a cap made of expensive silk shipped in from the Far East.

The shoes found at Coppergate were all made of leather but they came in a range of styles. Some had toggle fastenings. Some had drawstring laces and some were smartly decorated around the top with coloured thread.

Viking men wore a wool overtunic and trousers. If they were wealthy they wore a linen undertunic, too. A woolly Viking sock turned up at Jorvik but no Viking underwear has ever been found, so we don't know if they wore underpants.

Both men and women fastened their clothes with metal brooches. This selection was found at Jorvik.

We know that both men and women wore leather belts, hung with useful tools or pouches. In one Viking saga, a belt led to disaster. Two men were fighting and one man's trouser belt snapped. As he struggled to keep his trousers up, his enemy killed him!

Viking women wore a long under-dress and a wool pinafore tunic over the top, pinned at the shoulders with brooches. Vikings were skilled wool-weavers and coloured their yarn with natural plant dyes. They often edged their clothes with colourful woollen braids.

Think of some clothes you wear that would be familiar to the Vikings.

A Viking wise woman
THE LADY OF PEEL

Vikings made the Isle of Man their home, using Peel Harbour to shelter their longships. When a mysterious Viking woman was found buried in Peel, people admired her beautiful bead necklace and puzzled over the strange objects buried with her. She was nicknamed the Lady of Peel, but who was she and why was she buried with such unusual things?

950
Approximate date of burial

DATE FOUND:
1984, BY ARCHAEOLOGISTS.

PLACE FOUND:
PEEL, ISLE OF MAN.

The Lady of Peel was discovered in the grounds of Peel Castle, which was once the site of a Viking stronghold. Her grave was in a Christian cemetery, but though she was buried in a Christian spot the objects in her grave were definitely pagan. The people of the Isle of Man were Christians when the pagan Vikings arrived, but the two beliefs began to mix and eventually the Vikings became Christians, too. The Lady of Peel's grave is an example of the two beliefs existing side by side.

The Lady of Peel was buried lying on a feather pillow, wearing an amber pendant and a fine necklace of 70 beads. She had a pouch of small mysterious tools, along with knives, shears and a comb. She had a pestle and mortar for grinding up herbs and an ammonite fossil, which might have been a lucky charm for her.

The Isle of Man was ruled by the Kings of Norway until 1266. There are lots of Viking carvings scattered across the island, and other Viking burials, too.

The most mysterious object in the grave was an iron rod one metre long. It had been covered in different fabrics and a goose wing was laid on top of it. Rods like this have been found in other female graves in Scandinavia, but why? Viking carvings of magical figures carrying staffs have led to the idea that the rod might have been a wand used by pagan women to perform magical Viking rituals.

The Lady of Peel would have been important in her community if people thought she was a healer with magical powers. She certainly had a fine necklace made of unusual and valuable beads.

When the bones of the Lady of Peel were analysed, experts discovered that she was middle-aged and very unhealthy when she died. She suffered from rickets, which meant she had fragile bones and weak muscles. She was bow-legged, too.

What do you think the mysterious iron rod was for?

A Viking parliament
TYNWALD HILL

Vikings from across a region would meet up in summer to hold a Thing, a mass meeting to judge crimes, settle disputes and decide on new laws. The oldest continuous parliament in the world, the Isle of Man Tynwald, began as a Thing gathering in Viking times. The Thing was held on a man-made hill.

979
The first recorded Tynwald

DATE FOUND:
THE TYNWALD HAS NEVER GONE OUT OF USE!

PLACE FOUND:
TYNWALD HILL, ISLE OF MAN.

We know from historical records that the Vikings used to hold a Thing at the Tynwald, but its name is the biggest clue. It comes from Norse (Norwegian Viking) words meaning 'field of the meeting place'. There were other Thing sites around Britain but remains are hard to find. The best way to pinpoint them is to study old place names to find variations of the word 'thing'. Dingwall, Tingwall and Tinwald are locations we know of in Scotland. Thingwall was once

Vikings could swap news and even arrange marriages at a Thing. They would decide on new laws and settle any arguments. The Isle of Man Tynwald didn't always run smoothly, though. Violence occasionally broke out between rival groups of Vikings who argued with each other.

The Tynwald (shown below) is the oldest continuous parliament, but the earliest parliament in the world is thought to be the Viking Thingvellir, first held in Iceland in 930. It took place near the site shown here.

Modern parliaments owe some features to Viking Things. For instance, people stand up to argue their views before a new law is decided. The Isle of Man Parliament still meets on the four rings of Tynwald Hill every July.

People accused of crimes were brought before a Thing meeting and judged by a group of people similar to a modern jury. Criminals could be fined or even be declared a 'nithing' – an outlaw. A nithing was banished and banned from ever returning. Anyone who met him could kill him without being punished for murder.

Find out where people meet to pass laws in Britain today.

A Viking leader
ARDNAMURCHAN SHIP GRAVE

Viking leaders were powerful warriors with their own gang of fighting followers. When one of these leaders died they were given a special burial along with their weaponry. A warrior who died in western Scotland was so revered that he was given a burial in a Viking boat, perhaps to sail him to his afterlife.

900s
Approximate date of the burial

DATE FOUND:
2011, BY UNIVERSITY ARCHAEOLOGY STUDENTS.

PLACE FOUND:
ARDNAMURCHAN, HIGHLAND.

University archaeologists noticed a small mound of stones by the shore at Ardnamurchan. When they investigated they found that the stones had been carefully placed there. Underneath, an important warrior had been buried in a Viking boat that measured five metres long. His companions probably dragged it from the sea nearby and laid their dead leader inside it with his possessions.

Here is a reproduction of a Viking sword, which would have been a valuable object. Sometimes warriors even gave their swords names. *Leg Biter*, *War Flame* and *Life Taker* are examples we know of.

Underneath the stones (shown here) there was nothing left of the boat but rivets and a few wood fragments. There were only a couple of teeth and pieces of bone left from the man's body, but we know that he was buried with a shield on his chest and a sword, spear and axe by his side.

Archaeologists X-rayed the rust-encrusted sword and discovered that the blade was broken in several places. The warrior's companions probably did it, but we don't know why. It's possible they wanted to put it out of use in the human world but thought it would be whole in the afterlife.

Viking leaders based themselves in big thatched halls where their warriors and families lived, too. There they feasted after a battle or an animal hunt. We don't know where the dead warrior had his base, but we do know that his companions buried him with a drinking horn and cooking pots so he could feast in the afterlife.

If you were a Viking warrior with a sword, what would you call it?

The warrior's sword was buried with him because it would have been his prize possession. He also had a whetstone – a stone he would have used to sharpen his sword blade.

Hidden treasure
SILVERDALE HOARD

Buried treasure piles have been found around the Viking world. One of the biggest British finds, the Silverdale Hoard, was discovered hidden just below the surface of a Lancashire field. We'll never know for sure why the treasure was buried, but there are a few fascinating clues.

900
Approximate date of the hoard burial

DATE FOUND:
2011, BY A METAL DETECTORIST.

PLACE FOUND:
SILVERDALE, LANCASHIRE.

A local man struck lucky in Silverdale soon after his wife gave him a metal detector for Christmas. Just after he dropped his son off at school, and before he went to work, he thought he'd try it out in a field. There he discovered a lead container filled with over 200 pieces of Viking silver, mysteriously hidden over a thousand years ago.

The hoard (shown here) included silver armlets (bracelets), as well as rings, coins and chopped-up pieces of hack silver used as money. It's thought that the armlets probably came from Ireland.

There were coins from England, France, Scandinavia and even Iraq in the pile. One coin was a fake made of copper covered in a thin layer of silver.

The treasure was found with a metal detector similar to this one. When it was sold to a museum, the metal detectorist shared £110,000 with the farmer who owned the field where it was found.

We don't know why the Vikings sometimes buried treasure. Perhaps they just wanted to keep it safe. Another explanation for hoard-burying is found in one of the Viking saga stories. The hero of the saga buries some treasure to show off and get everyone talking about his wealth.

Around the time the Silverdale treasure was buried we know that Vikings were driven out of Dublin in Ireland, and they came to northern England. Perhaps they brought their wealth with them and buried it.

The Viking armlets look quite modern. Think of someone you know who wears similar bracelets.

Reading the runes
MAESHOWE

The Vikings had their own alphabet made up of letter symbols called runes. They used the runes to carve inscriptions on stones to commemorate the dead, and they also used it to carve graffiti. One of the best Viking graffiti collections in the world was found on the walls of an ancient tomb on Mainland, the largest of the Orkney Islands.

1153
Approximate date

DATE FOUND:
1861, BY AN AMATEUR ARCHAEOLOGIST.

PLACE FOUND:
MAESHOWE, MAINLAND, ORKNEY.

When an amateur archaeologist broke into the ancient Stone Age tomb of Maeshowe, he found that Vikings had been there centuries before him. They had carved graffiti on the walls with their knives and axes. A saga about the Orkney Vikings mentions a band of warriors sheltering in the old tomb during a terrible snowstorm in 1153. Perhaps they spent some of their time carving the messages.

We know that Ofram, Haermund, Thofin, Ottrfila, Tryggr and Arnfithr were among the graffiti artists because they all carved their names on the wall.

Runes are found carved on large rune stones set up across the Viking world to commemorate the lives of dead relatives. The runes were carved into the stone and then painted in bright colours.

Runes were sometimes made part of a picture. The runes shown here were carved inside the body of a snake-like monster on a Swedish rune stone.

Although the Vikings had an alphabet, they never wrote anything down on paper. We only know details about their history from the writings of their enemies, such as the Anglo-Saxons. Did their enemies always tell the truth about them? We don't know for sure!

From rune stone and graffiti clues, we know that many Vikings were well travelled. The runes sometimes describe faraway journeys or battles, and one famous piece of rune graffiti is in the church of Hagia Sophia in Istanbul, Turkey, very far from Scandinavia. Two Vikings, Halfdan and Arne, carved their tags in the church stone in the 800s.

People still write their names in graffiti. Where have you seen examples?

Viking pictures
ST. PAUL'S RUNE STONE

1030s
Approximate date

DATE FOUND:
1852, IN THE CHURCHYARD.

Viking art was zoomorphic, which means it showed magical animals. They were probably from Viking legends, and they were often shown wrapped around each other, fighting. One strange-looking animal fight was discovered right in the heart of London, in the churchyard of St. Paul's Cathedral.

PLACE FOUND:
CITY OF LONDON.

The St. Paul's Stone had been standing in the churchyard for hundreds of years when someone eventually realised what it was. It came from a time when a Viking king called Cnut took control of the whole of England. He was king from 1016 to 1035, and the stone may have commemorated one of the Viking followers who came to England with him. He was king of Denmark, Norway and part of Sweden, too.

The stone had traces of red, black and white paint on it, so we know it would once have been brightly decorated. It's thought to be a picture of a lion fighting a serpent.

Viking art has lots of swirling shapes in it. It shows creatures twisting around each other, and there are often lines of twisting pattern, too. This style is found on Viking jewellery, weapons and stone carving.

The stone was found in a Christian churchyard, but it had pagan-looking creatures on it. By the time Cnut ruled England many Vikings had converted to Christianity, but they saw no problem mixing up ideas from their new and old beliefs.

This Viking cross is in a churchyard in Gosforth, Cumbria. It is carved with Viking myths as well as scenes from the Bible.

From runes written around the sides of the stone we know that two people with Viking names – Ginna and Toki – had the stone made, but we don't know who it was for. Perhaps Ginna and Toki were the wife and son of someone who died.

Have a go at drawing a Viking-style picture of a fight between two animal monsters.

A new God
HORN OF ULF

How did a gigantic elephant tusk drinking horn belonging to a Viking end up in a Yorkshire cathedral (York Minster)? A generous Viking noble called Ulf gave it to the local monks, along with valuable land. Centuries later it was very nearly lost for good.

Early
1000s
Exact date unknown

DATE FOUND:
LOST IN 1640s
AND RETURNED
IN 1650s.

PLACE FOUND:
YORK MINSTER,
YORKSHIRE.

Ulf was a Viking noble who owned lands in the far north of England. He might have been a Danish Viking follower of King Cnut. We do know that he was no longer pagan because he decided to give his lands to the Christian church. It was a Danish tradition to hand over a drinking horn to seal a deal, so Ulf gave this fine one to the church at York.

The horn is made from an elephant's tusk, and it was probably carved in Salerno, Italy. It shows a unicorn and a gryphon (half lion, half eagle), along with a lion and wolves. The carving looks Middle Eastern and it was probably done by Iranian craftspeople. It was a luxury object and would have cost Ulf a lot of money.

A traditional local story tells of Ulf overhearing his ungrateful sons deciding how to split up his lands when he died. Disgusted by their attitude, he rode to York, filled his drinking horn with wine and knelt before the altar, promising his lands to God instead.

Centuries later, during the English Civil War (1642–1651), the horn was stolen from York Minster. After the war ended a local noble handed it back, explaining that he had found it and looked after it. Its Viking gold bands were missing, though, and instead someone had fitted it with silver bands. The Viking gold had probably been sold off.

This is a picture from the Bayeux Tapestry, showing how William the Conqueror took over England in 1066. William was descended from the Vikings, and he is an ancestor of the modern British Royal Family. In a way we could say that the Vikings (or at least their descendants) still rule!

Just a few decades after Ulf gave his gift, England was invaded by William of Normandy, known as William the Conqueror. The era of the Vikings and Anglo-Saxons was over in England, and the era of the Normans began. But the Isle of Man stayed Norwegian until 1266, and the Shetland Islands and Orkney were Danish until the 1400s.

If, like Ulf, you gave someone something you owned to seal an agreement, what would it be?

Glossary

altar   A holy table or platform in a church.

amber   Fossilised tree resin.

ammonite   An extinct sea animal with a coiled shell, related to squid.

Anglo-Saxon   People who settled in England before the Vikings came.

archaeologist   Someone who studies bones and the remains from human activity in the past.

Asgard   A kingdom in the sky where Viking gods and goddesses were thought to live.

Baltic   Countries that surround the Baltic Sea in northeast Europe.

commemorate   To do something to remember a dead person. The Vikings carved rune stones to commemorate their dead.

Danelaw   An area of English territory ruled over by Vikings, in agreement with the Anglo-Saxons.

Far East   Countries in east Asia.

Great Army   A big group of Vikings who came over to Britain in CE 865 and stayed, gradually conquering parts of the country.

hack silver   Scraps of silver that Vikings used as money, weighing the silver to decide its worth.

hoard   A hidden pile of treasure.

immortal   Living forever.

longhouse   A long building where Viking families lived together in one inside space.

longship   Seagoing Viking ship powered by oarsmen or with a sail.

massacre   The killing of many people.

Mercia   The Anglo-Saxon kingdom of central England.

monastery   A community of monks. In the time of the Vikings, monasteries were the home of Anglo-Saxon Christian monks in Britain.

nithing   A Viking outlaw. Becoming a nithing was a punishment for a crime.

Norse   The language spoken by the Vikings who arrived in Britain.

pagan   Someone who believes in many gods and goddesses, not the God of the Christian Bible.

pirate   Someone who attacks and robs others, usually from a ship.

priory   A small monastery.

prow   The front of a boat.

revered   Someone who is deeply respected or admired.

runes   Viking alphabet symbols.

saga   A Scandinavian story, telling a mythical tale.

scabbard   A sheath for a sword or knife.

shears   Very large scissors.

stern   The back of a boat.

Stone Age   The prehistoric time that lasted from around 3.5 million years ago to around 4,000 years ago.

truce   An agreement between enemies to stop fighting for a certain period of time.

Valhalla   A hall in the sky kingdom of Asgard, where Viking gods and goddesses lived. The hall was for warriors who fell in battle. They were said to feast and practise fighting there in the afterlife.

Wessex   The Anglo-Saxon kingdom of southern England.

yarn   A thread made from wool. The Vikings wove most of their clothing from wool yarn.

Further Information

WEBLINKS

jorvik-viking-centre.co.uk

Find out about the Viking finds in York and see a photo gallery of discoveries.

www.bbc.co.uk/history/ancient/vikings/launch_gms_viking_quest.shtml

Can you build a ship, cross the ocean, raid a monastery and return home with a prize? Play this online game to find out.

etc.ancient.eu/wp-content/uploads/2015/12/vikingrecepten2.pdf?212c3c

Authentic Viking recipes to try.

Note to parents and teachers: Every effort has been made by the Publishers to ensure that the websites in this book are suitable for children, that they are of the highest educational value, and that they contain no inappropriate or offensive material. However, because of the nature of the Internet, it is impossible to guarantee that the contents of these sites will not be altered. We strongly advise that Internet access is supervised by a responsible adult.

TIMELINE

CE 793 Vikings raided Lindisfarne Priory in Northumberland.

794 Vikings attacked Scotland.

800 Vikings farmed at Jarlshof on Mainland, Shetland, from around this time.

866 Vikings captured the town of York. They called it Jorvik. Many objects have been excavated from Viking times there.

873 The Viking Great Army camped at Repton in Derbyshire.

876 (Approx) Vikings from Denmark, Norway and Sweden began settling permanently in England.

889 King Alfred the Great agreed a boundary between his kingdom, Wessex, and land ruled by the Vikings – an area called the 'Danelaw'.

927 Athelstan of Wessex defeated a big force of Vikings and Scots to become the King of all Britain.

950 The Lady of Peel was buried on the Isle of Man.

954 The last Viking king of York was defeated.

970 (Approx) A group of Viking men were massacred at Ridgeway Hill, Weymouth.

979 The first recorded Tynwald meeting was held on the Isle of Man.

994 Vikings once again attacked southern Britain, besieging London.

1014 Viking King Cnut was crowned and became the first Scandinavian to rule England.

1066 William of Normandy conquered England, deposing the Anglo-Saxon rulers for good. He was of Viking descent.

1153 Vikings write graffiti on the tomb of Maeshowe on Mainland, Orkney.

Index

afterlife 6, 7, 20–21
amber 14, 17
amulets 7
Anglo-Saxons 5, 6, 7, 8, 9, 13, 25, 29
Ardnamurchan ship grave 20–21
art 10–11, 24–25, 26–27, 28, 29
Asgard 7

Bayeux Tapestry 29
bowls, wooden 12–13
brooches 14, 15

Christianity 5, 16, 27, 28
clothing 7, 8, 12, 14–15
Cnut, King 26, 27, 28
Coppergate 12–15
crimes 8, 18, 19
Cumbria 27

Danelaw 8
Denmark 6, 26
Derbyshire 6–7
Dorset 8–9

farmers/farming 10–11, 23
forensics 8

Gosforth Cross 27
graffiti 24–25

helmets 9
homes 10–11
Horn of Ulf 28–29
hunting 21

Iceland 19
Isle of Man 16–19, 29
Istanbul 25
Italy 28

Jarlshof 10–11
Jorvik 12–15

Lady of Peel 16–17
Lancashire 22–23
lawmaking 18–19
Lincolnshire 7
Lindisfarne 4–5
Lindisfarne Priory Stone 4–5
London 9, 26–27
longships 5, 9, 10–11, 16

Maeshow 24–25
metal detecting 22–23
monasteries 4–5

Normandy 29
Northumberland 4–5
Norway 17, 18, 26, 29

Orkney 24–25, 29
outlaws 19

Peel Harbour 16
Picts 10
pottery 12

raiding 4–5, 6
Repton 6–7
Ridgeway Hill

runes 24–25, 26–27
Russia 9

sagas 11, 15, 23, 24
Scandinavia 4, 9, 10, 17, 23, 25
Scotland 10–11, 18, 20–21, 24–25, 29
Shetland 10–11, 29
shoes 14–15
Silverdale Hoard 22–23
slaves 4, 5

teeth 9, 21
Thing 18–19
toys and games 11
treasure 4, 5, 22–23
Tynwald Hill 18–19

Viking Great Army 6–7

weapons 4–5, 6, 7, 20, 21, 24, 27
Weymouth 8–9
William the Conqueror 29
writing 5, 6, 25, 27

York 12–15, 28, 29
York Minster 28, 29
Yorkshire 12–15, 28